About the Author

Amanda M. Clarke is a celebrated author renowned for her insightful contributions to the field of divination and personal transformation. Her passion for writing blossomed early in life, primarily through poetry, but it was not until she navigated through a tumultuous 20-year marriage that she turned to Tarot, astrology, and angel cards. These tools not only offered her solace but also a path back to the aspirations of her youth.

Driven by her own journey and the limitations of traditional divination tools, Amanda shifted to writing, creating accessible guides that fit the modern seeker's lifestyle. Her works include the "Daily Guidance Series," featuring titles like "Vibes Unveiled," "Messages from the Angels," "Tarot Cat Oracles," and "Spirit Animal Oracle." Each book is designed for ease of use, perfect for quick, on-the-go insights during daily commutes or moments of stress.

Amanda's books are more than informational; they are companions in mindfulness, offering readers quick, reliable access to spiritual guidance. The act of flipping through the pages mimics the meditative practice of shuffling cards, providing a soothing, introspective experience. Through her writing, Amanda continues to empower and inspire those on a quest to enhance their lives, encouraging them to rediscover and reconnect with their innermost truths and strengths.

Disclaimer: The Angelic Oracles book provides information on spiritual readings and interpretation, but it is not intended as a substitute for professional advice, diagnosis, or treatment. The information contained in this book is provided for educational and entertainment purposes only and is not meant to be taken as specific advice for individual circumstances. The author and publisher make no representations or warranties with respect to the accuracy or completeness of the contents of this book and specifically disclaim any implied warranties of merchantability or fitness for a particular purpose. The reader should always consult with a licensed professional for any specific concerns or questions. The author and publisher shall not be liable for any loss or damage caused or alleged to have been caused, directly or indirectly, by the information contained in this book. The use of this book is at the reader's sole risk

The "Daily Guidance" series offers an innovative approach to finding spiritual wisdom and practical advice. Each book in the series is a unique tool designed for daily introspection and decision-making. Readers are invited to meditate on a question or seek general guidance for the day, then flip to a random page in the book. The page they land on provides a personalized message from various spiritual sources, such as angels, tarot, or spirit animals. With each turn of the page, these books deliver insightful, positive messages and mantras to inspire personal growth and provide clarity on life's daily challenges and decisions.

> ***Other books in this series:-***
> *Daily Angel Tarot Reading*
> *Mystic Tarot Cat*
> *Oracle of the Tarot Cat*
> *Vibes Unveiled*
> *Spirit Animal Oracle*
> *Answers from the Oracles*
> *Messages from the Angels*

More on the Bookshelves at www.korupublishing.com

The Angelic Oracle

Your Interactive Guide to Heavenly Messengers

Amanda M Clarke

Koru Lifestylist

KORU (Maori:NZ)
A symbol of spiritual growth and spiritual connection.

"The Angelic Oracle" by Amanda M. Clarke is a transformative journey into the realm of celestial wisdom, guided by the ethereal presence of angels. This unique book combines Amanda's profound insights with stunning AI-generated illustrations of the 95 angels, creating a visual and spiritual feast that enhances the reader's experience. Each page is adorned with captivating images that bring the angelic messages to life, making "The Angelic Oracles" not only a guide but a work of art. Designed for seekers of spiritual guidance, this book offers empowering, soothing, and enlightening messages from the angelic realm, making it a must-have for anyone looking to deepen their connection with the divine.

Copyright © 2024 by Koru Lifestylist

All rights reserved. All content, materials, and intellectual property in this book or any other platform owned by Koru Lifestylist are protected by copyright laws. This includes text, images, graphics, videos, audio, software, and any other form of content that may be produced by Koru Lifestylist.

No part of this content may be reproduced, distributed, or transmitted in any form or by any means without the prior written permission of Koru Lifestylist. This means that you cannot copy, reproduce, or use any of the content in this book for commercial or personal purposes without the express written consent of Koru Lifestylist.

Unauthorized use of any copyrighted material owned by Koru Lifestylist may result in legal action being taken against you. Koru Lifestylist reserves the right to pursue all available legal remedies against any individual or entity found to be infringing on its copyright.

In summary, Koru Lifestylist © 2024 holds exclusive rights to all the content produced by it, and any unauthorized use of such content will result in legal action.

Introduction to Angels

Angels, often depicted as messengers of the divine, have held a prominent place in many of the world's religions and spiritual traditions. Rooted in ancient scriptures and reinforced by centuries of folklore and theological study, angels are typically envisioned as celestial intermediaries, bridging the gap between the human and the divine. These beings, considered to be both powerful and benevolent, are believed to carry out God's will, deliver messages, offer guidance, and sometimes, provide protection to individuals.

The concept of angels as messengers is most prominently featured in monotheistic religions such as Christianity, Islam, and Judaism. In Christianity, angels are often seen as God's messengers who convey important messages to humans. One of the most famous biblical stories is that of the Archangel Gabriel announcing to the Virgin Mary that she would give birth to Jesus Christ. Similarly, in Islam, angels have a well-defined role, with Gabriel (Jibril in Arabic) revealing the Quran to the Prophet Muhammad over a period of 23 years. In Judaism, angels also serve as messengers, like in the story of the angel who stops Abraham from sacrificing his son Isaac.

Angels are typically depicted as pure spirits created by God, devoid of physical desires or needs, which allows them to focus solely on the will of God without distraction. They are often portrayed with wings, not necessarily to denote their ability to fly but as a symbol of their sublime nature and ability to traverse the celestial and earthly realms.

Furthermore, angels play a role in the spiritual life of individuals. Many people believe that angels can be called upon for guidance, comfort, and protection. This belief has permeated popular culture and spiritual practices, leading to the development of various modalities like angelic meditation, angel cards, and books focused on communication with angels.

In mystical and esoteric traditions, angels are sometimes considered to be manifestations of divine energy or specific aspects of God's creation, each responsible for different elements of the cosmos or human experience. Such interpretations allow for a broader understanding of angels, beyond just messengers to facilitators of the universal order.

Overall, the role of angels as messengers serves as a poignant reminder of the spiritual connection between the divine and the mundane, providing a source of comfort and inspiration for believers across different cultures and epochs. They symbolize the hope that there is something greater beyond our immediate perception, guiding and watching over humanity.

The Angelic Oracle

Welcome to "The Angelic Oracle: Your interactive guide to heavenly messengers," a spiritual companion designed to connect you with the celestial wisdom of 95 angels. This book is more than just a collection of messages; it is a portal to divine guidance, crafted to help you find answers to your life's questions and uncertainties.

Angels have long been revered as messengers and protectors, entities that bridge the divine and the human. Through the pages of this book, they extend their guidance to you, offering insights and affirmations that resonate with your spirit and circumstances. Each message is a whisper from the divine, tailored to the needs of your soul.

To fully embrace the potential of this book, begin with a mindset conducive to spiritual receptiveness. Consider starting each session with a brief meditation to center your thoughts and emotions. Sit comfortably, close your eyes, and take deep, steady breaths. Focus your attention on your Solar Plexus chakra (Manipura), which is located 1 to 2 inches above your naval. Envision it as a bright, spinning wheel of energy, radiating confidence and intuition.

With your question in mind, use this incantation to invoke the angels' presence:

> *"Angelic guardians, keepers of light,*
> *Hear my plea in this sacred rite.*
> *Guide my hand and bless my heart,*
> *Reveal the wisdom you impart."*

Hold the book in your hands, channeling your energy into its pages. When you feel ready, ask your question aloud or silently in your mind, then let the book fall open to a page. The message you find is the angels' response, tailored just for you. Trust that the answer is not only within these pages but also within your own intuition and the deep knowing of your Solar Plexus.

This book is your guide and your connection to the angelic realm. Let it lead you on a journey of discovery, where the answers you seek are revealed from within these pages, and self.

This book is dedicated to you
Barbara
a testament to the angel you were and the guardian you remain.

With enduring love and appreciation,

The Answers You Seek

Are Within

Poiel

"I am the angel of support and fortune. Remember, support often comes when least expected but most needed. Be open to receiving help, and equally ready to offer it. Your fortunes can change with simple acts of kindness and support. Embrace opportunities to be a pillar for others, and watch as the circle of support strengthens around you."

Poiel

"I give and receive support with grace."

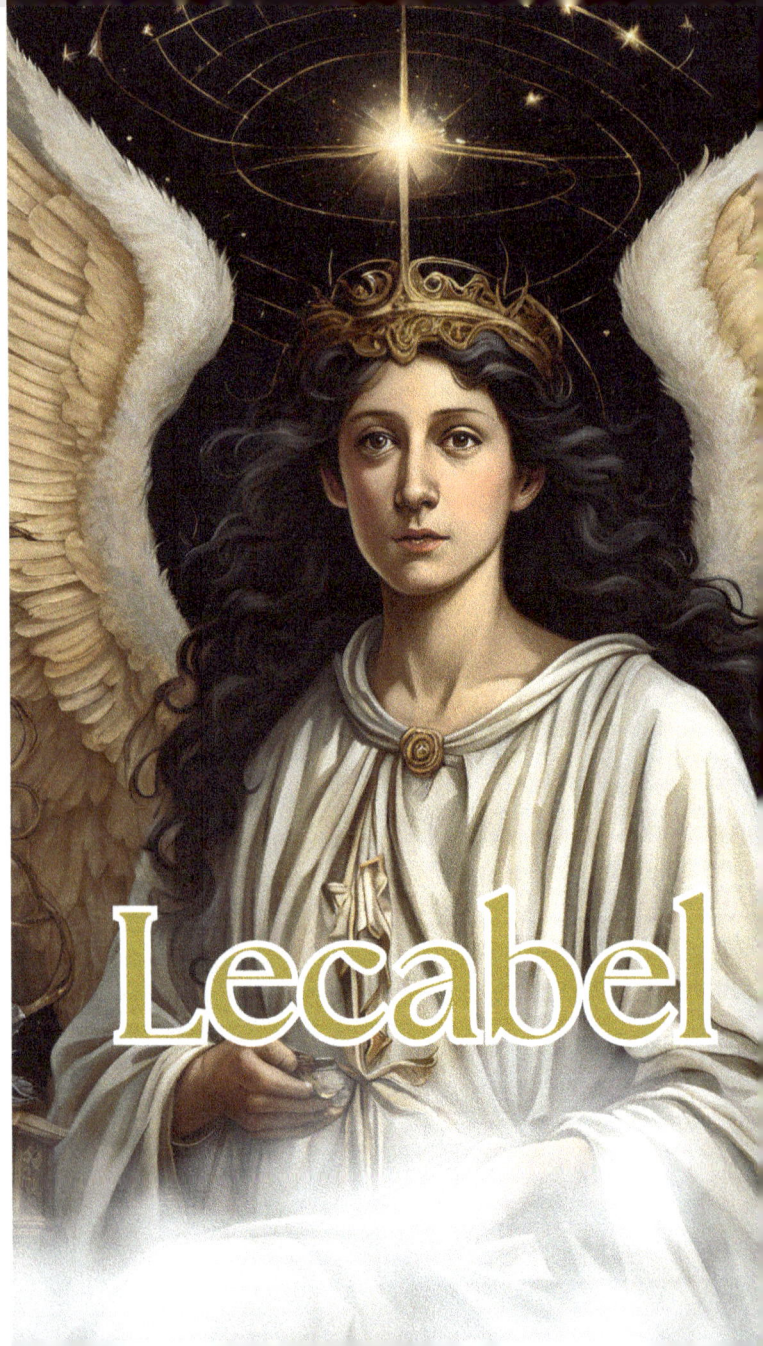

Lecabel

"As the angel of intellect and discovery, I urge you to pursue your curiosity and to embrace learning. Never stop asking questions and seeking answers. Your intellectual journey can lead to amazing discoveries that not only advance your understanding but also contribute to the world. Let knowledge empower you."

Lecabel

"Curiosity fuels my quest for knowledge."

Mehiel

"I am the angel of life and protection. Cherish and safeguard all forms of life around you, recognizing the sanctity of life in all its expressions. Stand as a protector of those who are vulnerable and extend your care and compassion to all beings. Your actions can be a beacon of hope and safety for others."

Mehiel

"I protect and cherish all life."

Kafziel

"Known as the angel of time and death, I remind you of the impermanence of life. Cherish each moment and live fully in the present. Use your time wisely, pursuing activities that bring joy and meaning to your life. Remember, time is a gift not to be wasted but to be utilized in fulfilling your life's purpose."

Kafziel

"I value and honor every moment."

Nathanael

"I am the angel of fire, representing transformation and renewal. Like the phoenix rising from its ashes, use the fires of challenges to forge strength and resilience. Embrace change and let it refine and define you, turning obstacles into opportunities for growth and enlightenment."

Nathanael

"Transformation through resilience and renewal."

Manakel

"As the angel of the ocean, I remind you of the depth and vastness of your own emotions. Dive deep into your feelings, understanding and embracing them. Like the ocean, your emotions have currents and depths that shape your experiences and interactions. Navigate them with care and respect, knowing they are a powerful force in your life."

Manakel

"I navigate the depths of my emotions with care."

Rochel

"I am the angel of restitution, encouraging you to restore what has been lost or taken unjustly. Whether it's returning a kindness or righting a wrong, your actions can heal and mend. Let fairness and honesty be your guides as you seek to set things right in your relationships and dealings."

Rochel

"I restore balance with fairness and honesty."

Barbiel

"Ruling the month of October and the sign of Scorpio, I bring transformation and depth to your life. Embrace the changes that come your way, diving deep into your emotions and experiences to unearth the truth. This period of introspection can lead to powerful self-discovery and renewal. Do not fear the depths, for within them lies the true treasure of personal growth and understanding."

Barbiel

"Transformation is my ally."

Amitiel

"I bring the truth to light, encouraging you to seek honesty in your dealings and to be true to yourself. Embrace transparency in your actions and thoughts, for this will lead you to a path of clarity and light. Let truth guide your decisions, and allow it to be the bedrock upon which your integrity is built. In knowing and facing the truth, you find genuine freedom and peace."

Amitiel

"Truth guides my path."

Verchiel

"I govern those born under the sign of Leo, inspiring leadership and the courage to shine brightly. Lead with heart and strength, letting your actions inspire others to follow their own paths with confidence. Embrace the spotlight when it finds you, using it to highlight causes dear to your heart."

Verchiel

"I lead with heart and inspire others."

Zaphkiel

"I am the angel of contemplation and reflection. Take time to reflect on your life, considering both your successes and your learning moments. Contemplation allows you to gain deeper insights and to grow in wisdom. Let reflection guide your future actions, making them more thoughtful and effective."

Zaphkiel

"Reflection deepens my wisdom and guides my actions."

Mumiah

"I oversee endings and longevity, reminding you that every ending is a new beginning. Embrace the completion of phases in your life as opportunities for renewal and growth. Reflect on your experiences, learn from them, and move forward with wisdom. Remember, life's cycles are a reflection of the eternal balance of endings and beginnings."

Mumiah

"Every ending is a new beginning."

Kokabiel

"As the angel of the stars, I guide you to find guidance in the celestial patterns. Let the stars inspire you with their beauty and mystery. Just as they guide sailors and travelers, let them remind you of your own journey through life. Look up and dream big, for the universe is vast and full of possibilities."

Kokabiel

"The stars guide me on my journey."

Ecanus

"I am the angel of writers and teachers, guiding those who seek to spread knowledge and wisdom. Embrace your role as a communicator, whether through words, art, or teaching. Share your knowledge generously, and in doing so, educate, inspire, and enlighten others. Your words and ideas have the power to effect change and foster understanding across boundaries."

Ecanus

"Knowledge to inspire and enlighten."

Dalquiel

"As a prince of the third heaven, I oversee the realms of higher understanding and spiritual elevation. Seek to elevate your soul by connecting with the divine. Let your spiritual practices guide you to higher planes of existence, where peace and understanding reign. In your quest for spiritual growth, remember that the journey is as significant as the destination."

Dalquiel

"Elevation through spirituality."

Nitika

"Angel of precious stones, I remind you of the hidden treasures within you and others. Like the gemstones buried deep within the earth, your inner strengths and qualities are valuable and unique. Recognize and cultivate your inner resources, and see the value in those around you as well."

Nitika

"I recognize and value the hidden treasures within."

Rikbiel

"As the angel of divine will, I guide you to align your desires with the divine purpose. Seek to understand your higher calling and let this knowledge guide your actions and choices. When your will is in harmony with the divine, your actions become more impactful and your life more fulfilling."

Rikbiel

"My will aligns with the divine."

Soqedhozi

"Keeper of the divine balance, I remind you of the importance of balance in all aspects of your life. Strive for equilibrium between work and rest, giving and receiving, action and contemplation. A balanced life respects the various aspects of your being and promotes a harmonious existence."

Soqedhozi

"Balance in all things is my goal."

Tagas

"Guardian of the gates of the south wind, I bring warmth and renewal. Embrace the warmth of new opportunities and the fresh breath of inspiration. Let the south wind carry away old woes and breathe new life into your endeavors. Welcome change like a warm breeze that rejuvenates your soul."

Tagas

"I welcome change with warmth and openness."

Yabamiah

"As the angel of alchemy and transformation, I remind you that you have the power to transform your life and your surroundings. Like the alchemist turns lead into gold, you can turn challenges into opportunities and pain into strength. Embrace the transformative power within you and around you."

Yabamiah

"I transform my life with alchemy of the spirit."

Rathanael

"I am the angel of law, reminding you of the importance of order and justice in your life. Uphold principles of fairness and lawfulness in all your dealings. Your adherence to justice not only shapes your character but also influences the community around you. Be a beacon of integrity and righteousness."

Rathanael

"Justice and law guide my actions."

Pahaliah

"Angel of redemption, I guide you to seek redemption and moral integrity in your life. Reflect on your values and align your actions with them. Strive for a life that reflects your highest ethical standards, and seek to make amends where necessary. Your pursuit of integrity is a journey towards spiritual fulfillment."

Pahaliah

"I seek redemption through integrity."

Puriel

"As the angel of punishment and purification, I remind you of the importance of accountability and self-reflection. Acknowledge your missteps and learn from them. Purification comes through the acceptance of responsibility and the commitment to personal growth. Let each lesson refine your soul and guide your actions."

Puriel

"I embrace growth through accountability."

Lahabiel

"Protector against evil spirits, I empower you to shield yourself from negativity. Use tools of spiritual protection, such as prayer, meditation, and positive affirmations. Surround yourself with people who uplift and support you. Remember, your spiritual shield is as strong as your belief and will."

Lahabiel

"I am protected by light and love."

Gavreel

"I am the angel of peace, here to remind you that peace begins within. Cultivate inner peace through meditation, reflection, and forgiveness. As you find peace in your heart, extend it to others in your interactions. Your calm presence can soothe troubled waters and bring harmony to those around you. Let peace be your guide in all your relationships and endeavors."

Gavreel

"Inner peace leads to world peace."

Charoum

"I stand as a guardian of the environment, reminding you of your responsibility to care for the earth. Each choice you make impacts your surroundings, so choose wisely. Engage in practices that sustain and regenerate the natural world. Your efforts to live sustainably are an act of respect not only for nature but for future generations as well."

Charoum

"I sustain the earth."

Ariel

"As a guardian of nature, I encourage you to protect and cherish the natural world around you. Your actions have a profound impact on the earth and its creatures. Show compassion and respect for all living things, and take steps to preserve the beauty and health of your environment. Through your care, you contribute to the balance and well-being of the planet. fostering a connection that nourishes your own spirit."

Ariel

"I honor and protect nature."

Nahaliel

"As the angel of rivers, I remind you of the importance of flow and adaptability in your life. Like a river, life has its bends and currents. Embrace the flow of your experiences, adapting to changes with grace and resilience. Let your life flow naturally, finding paths through the obstacles you encounter."

Nahaliel

"I flow with grace through life's currents."

Uzziel

"I am the angel of faith and courage. In moments of doubt, remember that faith is your shield and courage your sword. Trust in the higher powers and in your own abilities. Let your faith be strong and your actions brave, as you face the uncertainties of life."

Uzziel

"Faith and courage lead my way."

Seheiah

"I am the angel of longevity and protection. Embrace practices that promote your well-being and longevity. Care for your physical and mental health as you would a precious gift. Protect yourself from harm through wise choices and proactive measures. Your health is a cornerstone of a long and fulfilling life."

Seheiah

"I protect my health for a long, fulfilling life."

Iofiel

"Beauty of God, I inspire appreciation for beauty in all its forms. Notice the beauty around you, in nature, art, and people. Let it uplift and inspire you. Create beauty in your own life, whether through creativity, kindness, or simplicity. Recognize that beauty exists not only in what is seen but also in feelings and experiences."

Iofiel

"Beauty surrounds me and is within me."

Camael

"As the angel of strength and courage, I am here to remind you that your inner strength is greater than any challenge you might face. Call upon your courage, and face your fears head-on. Each step taken in bravery is a step towards conquering your fears and achieving your goals. You are stronger than you know, and with each act of courage, you grow even stronger."

Camael

"Strength and courage define me."

Anahel

"As the angel who moves the heavenly spheres, I remind you of the endless cycles and rhythms that govern the cosmos and your life. Align yourself with these natural rhythms, respecting the ebb and flow of energy within and around you. Let harmony and balance be your guides, as you navigate through life's ups and downs. Embrace change as it comes, for each phase of life brings new opportunities."

Anahel

"I flow with cosmic rhythms."

Jehoel

"As the guardian of the divine throne, I invite you to seek a closer connection with the divine. Let your spiritual pursuits be guided by a desire to feel closer to the Creator. Practice humility and reverence in your spiritual life, and find joy in the sacred connection that you forge through your faith and devotion."

Jehoel

"Closer to the divine each day."

Harahel

"I oversee libraries and archives, encouraging you to seek wisdom in the knowledge of the past. Delve into history and literature to understand more about the world and yourself. Let the lessons of history guide your decisions, and allow the stories of others to inspire and teach you. Knowledge is a treasure that grows when shared."

Harahel

"Wisdom of the past enlightens my future."

Stamiel

"I am the angel of sacred silence and inner listening. In the quiet moments, listen deeply to your inner voice and the whispers of the divine. Sacred silence is a source of great wisdom and peace. Cultivate moments of stillness in your life to connect more deeply with your true self and the universe."

Stamiel

"In silence, I find wisdom."

Vehuel

"As the angel of elevation and grandeur, I encourage you to aspire to greater heights in your spiritual and personal life. Seek grandeur not in material possessions but in the richness of your experiences and the depth of your relationships. Elevate your thoughts and actions to reflect the highest ideals."

Vehuel

"I aspire to elevate my spirit and actions."

Tzadkiel

"As the angel of justice and freedom, I inspire you to stand up for what is right and to seek freedom for yourself and others. Your actions can create ripples of justice and liberation. Let fairness guide your decisions, and fight for the freedom of those who cannot."

Tzadkiel

"I advocate for justice and freedom."

Sorath

"As the angel who governs the inferno, I remind you that even in the darkest moments, there is a force that can guide you to light. Embrace the transformative power of challenges, seeing them as opportunities to grow and strengthen your spirit. Face your fears and adversities with courage, and let your resilience shine through."

Sorath

"I transform challenges into growth."

Jibril

"The Islamic name for Gabriel. I bring messages of significant change and divine wisdom. Be open to receiving divine knowledge, and let it guide you in your decisions, ensuring they serve a greater good."

Jibril

"Divine wisdom guides my decisions."

Nemamiah

"This guardian angel of great generals, I inspire leadership and strategic thinking. Lead with integrity and courage, inspiring those around you. Be strategic in your decisions, thinking ahead and preparing for various outcomes. Your leadership can guide others through challenges and toward success."

Nemamiah

"I lead with integrity and strategic foresight."

Mihr

"As the angel of friendship and love, I encourage you to cultivate meaningful relationships. Cherish your friends and loved ones, recognizing the strength that love and friendship bring to your life. Be open, honest, and supportive in your relationships, fostering connections that are built on trust and mutual respect."

Mihr

"Love and friendship guide my way."

Omniel

"This angel overcomes difficulties, reminding you that you too have the strength to overcome the challenges you face. Embrace resilience and persistence as your tools. Each difficulty you face is an opportunity to grow stronger and more adept at navigating life's complexities."

Omniel

"I overcome difficulties with strength and resilience."

Rehael

"As the angel of obedience, I encourage you to consider the value of discipline and respect for authority when it is just and moral. Obedience to these principles can bring structure and stability to your life. Reflect on the sources of authority you choose to follow, ensuring they align with your highest values."

Rehael

"Discipline and respect bring order to my life."

Boamiel

"Though less known, my presence in your life is marked by the blessings of the lesser-seen wonders. Look closer at the small joys and simple pleasures; therein lies the beauty of life. Appreciate the quiet moments and the subtle elements that bring depth to your daily experiences. Find joy in the unnoticed, for they are the foundation of a fulfilled life."

Boamiel

"Joy in every small wonder."

Sealiah

"As the angel of motivation and willpower, I empower you to pursue your goals with determination. Let your inner strength be the wind at your back, pushing you towards your aspirations. Stay motivated even in the face of adversity, and use your willpower to overcome obstacles."

Sealiah

"Determination drives my journey toward success."

Sofiel

"As the angel of nature, I remind you of the beauty and wisdom that nature holds. Spend time in natural settings to reconnect with the earth and its cycles. Let the simplicity of nature teach you about growth, renewal, and the natural flow of life. Nature is both a sanctuary and a teacher."

Sofiel

"Nature teaches and nurtures me."

Penemue

"I taught mankind the art of writing, thus opening doors to expression and communication. Embrace the power of words to share knowledge, inspire change, and express your innermost thoughts and feelings. Writing can be a tool for healing, discovery, and connection. Let your words flow freely and truthfully, creating bridges between hearts and minds."

Penemue

"My words inspire, heal, and connect."

Tzaphkiel

"Associated with contemplation and understanding. I encourage you to engage in deep thought and seek understanding in all aspects of your life. Through contemplation, you can achieve greater insight into your challenges and experiences, leading to profound wisdom and inner peace."

Tzaphkiel

"Contemplation brings understanding and peace."

Haniel

"I am associated with grace and beauty, reminding you to approach life with grace in your actions and to appreciate the beauty that surrounds you and is within you. Cultivate a life that reflects beauty in kindness, creativity, and compassion. Let grace be your guide in difficult times and your constant companion in all others."

Haniel

"Grace and beauty guide my every step."

Ramiel

"Often seen as an angel of hope and mercy, I bring you reassurance in times of despair. Hold onto hope even in the darkest moments, for it is the beacon that will guide you through. Show mercy to yourself and others, creating a ripple of comfort and relief in a world in need."

Ramiel

"Hope and mercy are my guides."

Dumah

"As an angel of silence and the stillness of death, I remind you of the importance of quiet reflection and the inevitable end that comes to all life. Embrace silence to hear your inner voice more clearly and remember that in the stillness, profound truths are often discovered."

Dumah

"Silence teaches me profound truths."

Mikail

"The Islamic name for Michael, I offer protection and deliverance from hardship. Trust in divine protection as you face life's challenges. Call upon your faith to shield you, and let your spirit be fortified by this trust."

Mikail

"My faith protects and strengthens me."

Gadreel

"Though known for leading astray, I also represent the potential for redemption and learning from one's errors. Reflect on your mistakes as stepping stones towards greater understanding and personal growth. Allow every misstep to teach you and guide you closer to your true path."

Gadreel

"I learn and grow from each misstep."

Jerahmeel

"Recognized for divine mercy, I encourage you to practice compassion and understanding towards others. Mercy enriches the giver and receiver alike, fostering an environment of forgiveness and healing. Let mercy lead your actions, smoothing the rough edges of human interaction."

Jerahmeel

"Mercy and compassion rule my actions."

Lailah

"As the overseer of conception and childbirth, I remind you of the miracle of life and the new beginnings it represents. Cherish and protect the newness in all forms, be it a child, an idea, or a journey. Every beginning holds the promise of growth and discovery."

Lailah

"I honor and protect all new beginnings."

Mastema

"Often leading evil spirits to test faith, I remind you that adversity is a tool for strengthening resolve and virtue. Embrace challenges as opportunities to fortify your faith and clarify your convictions. Let each trial polish your spirit to a finer shine."

Mastema

"Adversity strengthens my faith and resolve."

Nuriel

"As the angel of hailstorms and thunder, I embody the tumultuous and transformative power of nature. Respect the might of natural forces and let them remind you of your own inner strength and resilience. Just as storms transform the landscape, let life's challenges transform you for the better."

Nuriel

"I find strength and transformation in life's storms."

Azrael

"As the angel of death, I remind you of life's impermanence and the importance of living each day with purpose and kindness. Reflect on the legacy you wish to leave behind and strive to make a positive impact in the lives of others. Understand that while physical existence is transient, the spirit and the deeds live on."

Azrael

"I live each day with purpose and kindness."

Jophiel

"Associated with beauty and wisdom, I inspire you to see the beauty in all things and to cultivate a beautiful mind. Seek knowledge that enriches your soul and look for beauty in everyday life. Let these pursuits elevate your spirit and brighten the world around you."

Jophiel

"Beauty and wisdom enrich my life."

Chamuel

"As an angel of peace and comfort, I encourage you to be a source of tranquility and reassurance in a tumultuous world. Spread peace through your words and actions. Comfort those in distress, and strive to create environments where peace and harmony flourish."

Chamuel

"I am a beacon of peace and comfort."

Zadkiel

"Sometimes known for mercy and forgiveness, I remind you of the power of compassion. Extend forgiveness to those who have wronged you and seek reconciliation where possible. Let mercy guide your judgments, allowing room for growth and healing in relationships."

Zadkiel

"Mercy and forgiveness guide my actions."

Barachiel

"Associated with blessings and guidance, I encourage you to recognize and appreciate the blessings in your life, both big and small. Share your blessings with others, and be a guide to those seeking direction. Your kindness can lead the way to a brighter path for many."

Barachiel

"I recognize and share my blessings."

Anael

"Associated with love, sexuality, and reproduction, I inspire you to embrace and honor love in all its forms. Cultivate loving relationships that are respectful and nurturing. Celebrate the creative power of love, which brings new life and joy into the world."

Anael

"Love in all its forms enriches my life."

Cassiel

"Known as the angel of solitude and tears, I remind you of the value of introspection and the catharsis of emotional expression. Embrace moments of solitude to reflect and heal. Let your tears cleanse the soul, allowing you to face the world with renewed strength."

Cassiel

"Solitude and reflection renew my spirit."

Sachiel

"Associated with wealth and charity, I encourage you to be generous with your resources and kindness. Wealth is not measured only by material possessions but also by the richness of your spirit. Share generously, and your life will be abundant in ways that matter most."

Sachiel

"Generosity enriches my life and others'."

Sariel

"Often linked with guidance and fate, I remind you that while some paths are destined, many are shaped by your choices. Seek divine guidance to navigate life's complexities and make decisions that align with your highest good. Trust in the journey, even when the destination is not yet clear."

Sariel

"Guidance and choice shape my destiny."

Raziel

"As the keeper of secrets and the angel of mysteries, I inspire you to delve into the deeper mysteries of life and the universe. Cultivate a sense of wonder and curiosity. The pursuit of hidden knowledge can lead to profound understanding and spiritual growth."

Raziel

"Mysteries of the universe guide my growth."

Michael

"As a protector and the leader of the army of God, I encourage you to stand firm in the face of adversity and defend the good with courage and strength. Let integrity and justice be your armor, and let compassion guide your actions as you battle against the forces of evil. Remember, true strength lies in righteousness and bravery."

Michael

"I defend the good with courage and integrity."

Gabriel

"As a messenger of God, I bring news of great importance and guide you in understanding divine messages. Listen closely to the whispers of the divine, and let clarity and truth guide your path. Embrace the role of a communicator who spreads wisdom and truth in a world that thirsts for genuine understanding."

Gabriel

"Divine messages guide my words and actions."

Raphael

"I am tasked with healing and providing divine providence. Call upon me when you need healing, whether physical, emotional, or spiritual. Let your heart be open to healing, and trust in the divine process that restores wholeness. Act as a healer in your own world, spreading kindness and care wherever you go."

Raphael

"Healing flows through me and from me."

Uriel

"As the angel associated with wisdom, I illuminate your path with insight and clarity. Seek wisdom in all your endeavors; let it be the light that guides you through darkness. Ask for understanding, and be willing to learn from every situation you face. Let wisdom be your compass."

Uriel

"Wisdom illuminates my path."

Samael

"Often seen as an angel of death or a stern judge, I remind you of the importance of accountability. Face the consequences of your actions with courage, and let integrity guide your decisions. Understand that every end is also a beginning, and transformation is often born from the ashes of the past."

Samael

"Accountability and transformation guide me."

Lucifer

"Known for the narrative of the fallen angel, I symbolize the dual nature of light and darkness. Understand that knowledge and power come with responsibility. Strive to use your insights and abilities wisely, aiming always to uplift and enlighten rather than mislead or control."

Lucifer

"I use knowledge wisely and responsibly."

Metatron

"As an archangel in Judaism, I record the deeds of humanity. Remember that your actions write the story of your life. Let each deed reflect the best of your spirit and character. Strive to live a life that, when recorded, tells a story of love, service, and integrity."

Metatron

"My deeds reflect my best self."

Sandalphon

"I carry the prayers of the faithful to God. Let your prayers be sincere and heartfelt, reaching out with true desire for connection and transformation. Pray not only for yourself but for the betterment of the world. Your prayers are a bridge between Earth and the Divine."

Sandalphon

"My prayers connect and transform."

Raguel

"Known as the angel of justice and fairness, I encourage you to seek equity and fairness in all your interactions. Let justice be the foundation of your relationships and endeavors. Stand up for fairness, not only for yourself but for those who lack voice and power."

Raguel

"Justice and fairness guide my every interaction."

Remiel

"I guide the souls of the faithful to heaven. Let your life be a journey toward spiritual ascension. Live in such a way that your soul moves ever closer to the divine, filled with peace, love, and righteousness. Be a guiding light for others on their spiritual paths as well."

Remiel

"I aspire to spiritual ascension and guide others."

Israfil

"I am Israfil, tasked with sounding the trumpet at the end of time in Islamic tradition. I remind you of the impermanence of the world and the importance of living a righteous life. Each moment is precious: live it in a way that honors your deepest values and prepares you for any eventual reckoning. Let your deeds reflect your faith and integrity."

Israfil

"I live each moment with integrity and faith."

Munkar

"As one who tests the faith of the dead, I remind you of the scrutiny that beliefs undergo after life. Cultivate a faith that withstands trials and tribulations, rooted deeply in truth and compassion. Live a life that you can defend with pride at its end."

Munkar

"My faith is strong and rooted in truth."

Nakir

"Working alongside Munkar, I also test the faith of the deceased. Remember, your beliefs are shown not just in words but in actions. Let your actions throughout life be a testament to your faith and values. Integrity in life leads to peace in death."

Nakir

"I act in ways that reflect my deepest beliefs."

Ophanim

"We are the celestial beings in wheel-like form, embodying the constant motion of the cosmos. Embrace change as an essential aspect of life, continuously moving and evolving. Let the journey inspire as much as the destination."

Ophanim

"I embrace the perpetual motion of life."

Seraphim

"As the highest order of angels, we stand closest to the divine fire. Strive to elevate your soul through purity, worship, and dedication to spiritual growth. Let your life be a flame that burns brightly in devotion."

Seraphim

"My spirit burns bright with devotion and purity."

Cherubim

"We guard the sacred spaces and the way to the divine. Protect your inner sanctum—your mind and spirit—from negative influences. Cultivate a sacred space within you that nurtures your spiritual growth."

Cherubim

"I protect my spirit and cultivate my inner sanctuary."

Principality

"We oversee nations and leaders, reminding you of the importance of governance that aligns with divine principles. Strive for leadership that embodies justice, mercy, and truth, whether in large realms or small personal domains."

Principality

"I lead with justice, mercy, and truth."

Archangel

"As God's messengers, we deliver divine decrees and inspire humans towards their higher callings. Be receptive to the messages that guide you, and act upon them with courage and conviction."

Archangel

"I listen and act on divine guidance."

Virtue

"We are associated with miracles and God's blessings. Remember that miracles are not only grand events but also small, everyday occurrences that affirm the divine presence in your life. Recognize and appreciate these blessings daily."

Virtue

"I recognize and cherish daily miracles."

Power

"We maintain order and harmony in the cosmos. Emulate this order in your life by creating balance and harmony in your relationships and environments. Let your life reflect the cosmic order through peace and stability."

Power

"Harmony and order govern my life."

Dominion

"Tasked with regulating the duties of angels, we remind you of the importance of responsibility and accountability in all endeavors. Take charge of your roles diligently, ensuring that your actions align with your moral and spiritual values."

Dominion

"I fulfill my responsibilities with integrity."

Throne

"As beings who act as God's chariot, we represent divine authority and sovereignty. Embrace your own authority by living in alignment with your highest truth and moral compass. Let your life be a testament to your authentic power."

Throne

"I live authentically and embrace my personal power."

Malik

"In Islam, I am the guardian of Hell, a role that underscores the consequences of one's life choices. Reflect deeply on your actions and their impacts, striving always to choose paths that lead to peace and righteousness."

Malik

"I choose actions that lead to peace."

Ridwan

"As the keeper of paradise in Islam, I remind you of the rewards that await those who live righteously. Strive for a life of virtue, keeping your eyes on the eternal rewards of your good deeds."

Ridwan

"I strive for virtue and look to eternal rewards."

Harut

"Sent to Earth to test humanity's faith, I remind you that every challenge tests and refines your beliefs. Engage with challenges not as obstacles, but as opportunities to deepen your understanding and strengthen your faith."

Harut

"Challenges refine and strengthen my faith."

Marut

"I test the moral fiber of humanity. Remember, every decision shapes your character. Make choices that reflect your highest ethical standards and contribute positively to the world around you."

Marut

"My choices reflect my ethics and integrity."

Izra'il

"Another name for Azrael, the angel of death, reminding you of life's transience. Live each day fully, knowing that each moment is precious. Let the knowledge of life's impermanence inspire you to live with purpose and love."

Izra'il

"I live fully, embracing each precious moment."

www.ingramcontent.com/pod-product-compliance
Lightning Source LLC
Chambersburg PA
CBHW042343300426
44109CB00049B/2758